HOW TO GET (AND KEEP) MORE MONEY

Eddie Powell, MBA
DBA Candidate, D.D.

To get started, let's get the disclaimer and legal stuff out of the way.

DISCLAIMER AND TERMS OF USE AGREEMENT

The author and publisher of this report and the accompanying materials have used their best efforts in preparing this report.

The author and publisher make no representation or warranties with respect to the accuracy, applicability, fitness, or completeness of the contents of this report.

The information contained in this report is strictly for educational purposes. Obviously, contact legal and/or financial professionals to assist you in any endeavor.

Therefore, if you wish to apply ideas contained in this report, you are taking full responsibility for your actions.

EVERY EFFORT HAS BEEN MADE TO ACCURATELY REPRESENT THIS PRODUCT AND IT'S POTENTIAL. EVEN THOUGH THIS INDUSTRY IS ONE OF THE FEW WHERE ONE CAN WRITE THEIR OWN CHECK IN TERMS OF EARNINGS, THERE IS NO GUARANTEE THAT YOU WILL EARN ANY MONEY USING THE TECHNIQUES AND IDEAS IN THESE MATERIALS. EXAMPLES IN THESE MATERIALS ARE NOT TO BE INTERPRETED AS A PROMISE OR GUARANTEE OF EARNINGS.

EARNING POTENTIAL IS ENTIRELYDEPENDENT ON THE PERSON USING OUR PRODUCT, IDEAS AND TECHNIQUES. WE DO NOT PURPORT THIS AS A "GET RICH SCHEME."

ANY CLAIMS MADE OF ACTUAL EARNINGS OR EXAMPLES OF ACTUAL RESULTS CAN BE VERIFIED UPON REQUEST. YOUR LEVEL OF SUCCESS IN ATTAINING THE RESULTS CLAIMED IN OUR MATERIALS DEPENDS ON THE TIME YOU DEVOTE TO THE PROGRAM, IDEAS AND TECHNIQUES MENTIONED, YOUR FINANCES, KNOWLEDGE AND VARIOUS SKILLS. SINCE THESE FACTORS DIFFER ACCORDING TO INDIVIDUALS, WE CANNOT GUARANTEE YOUR SUCCESS OR INCOME LEVEL. NOR ARE WE RESPONSIBLE FOR ANY OF YOUR ACTIONS.

MATERIALS IN OUR PRODUCT AND OUR WEBSITE MAY CONTAIN INFORMATION THAT INCLUDES OR IS BASED UPON FORWARD - LOOKING STATEMENTS WITHIN THE MEANING OF THE SECURITIES LITIGATION REFORM ACT OF 1995.

FORWARD - LOOKING STATEMENTS GIVE OUR EXPECTATIONS OR FORECASTS OF FUTURE EVENTS. YOU CAN IDENTIFY THESE STATEMENTS BY THE FACT THAT THEY DO NOT RELATE STRICTLY TO HISTORICAL OR CURRENT FACTS. THEY USE WORDS SUCH AS "ANTICIPATE," "ESTIMATE," "EXPECT," "PROJECT," "INTEND," "PLAN," "BELIEVE," AND OTHER WORDS AND TERMS OF SIMILAR MEANING IN CONNECTION WITH A DESCRIPTION OF POTENTIAL EARNINGS OR FINANCIAL PERFORMANCE. ANY AND ALL FORWARD LOOKING STATEMENTS HERE OR ON ANY OF OUR SALES MATERIAL ARE INTENDED TO EXPRESS OUR OPINION OF EARNINGS POTENTIAL. MANY FACTORS WILL BE IMPORTANT IN DETERMINING YOUR ACTUAL RESULTS AND NO GUARANTEES ARE MADE THAT YOU WILL ACHIEVE RESULTS SIMILAR TO OURS OR ANYBODY ELSES, IN FACT NO GUARANTEES ARE MADE THAT YOU WILL ACHIEVE ANY RESULTS FROM OUR IDEAS AND TECHNIQUES IN OUR MATERIAL.

The author and publisher disclaim any warranties (express or implied), merchantability, or fitness for any particular purpose. The author and publisher shall in no event be held liable to any party for any direct, indirect, punitive, special, incidental or other consequential damages arising directly or indirectly from any use of this material, which is provided "as is", and without warranties.

As always, the advice of a competent legal, tax, accounting or other professional should be sought.

The author and publisher do not warrant the performance, effectiveness or applicability of any sites listed or linked to in this report. All links are for information purposes only and are not warranted for content, accuracy or any other implied or explicit purpose.

HOW TO GET (AND KEEP) MORE MONEY

The 3 Secret Keys Revealed

By: Eddie Powell, MBA, DBA Candidate, D.D.

Today it seems that nearly everyone is trying to get and keep more money. Some are trying an experts system of hidden mind control techniques, others are getting themselves hypnotized, and yet others are stumbling around just looking in the seats of the couch for any little bit of small change they can find.

Now, don't get me wrong, I have been there – right there with you! I know what it is like to be on unemployment searching for another job but nothing happens. I know what it is like to count slices of bologna to see if we can make it until Tuesday. I know what it is like to have unexpected car trouble while still trying to feed the family and just make it through.

You see, you and I are a lot alike. We just hadn't met yet. But, now that you're here, I am delighted to share with you what I learned from the School of Hard Knocks and perhaps save you a tremendous amount of time, stress, and let you know that there is hope, an answer to all this.

HOW TO GET (AND KEEP) MORE MONEY and EDDIE POWELL'S QUANTUM LEAP BUSINESS TRAINING © 2010 Shared Resource Network, Inc., POB 65, Reynoldsburg, OH 43068-0065 USA   All World Rights Reserved. 6
Eddie@EddiePowell.com

I call it The 3 Secret Keys of How To Get And Keep More Money!

Before we go there, please allow me to share my story for a moment. Like many people, I have had a few careers in my lifetime. I have been in entertainment, radio, television, education, and more. The great part has been the highs I get from being at the top of my game, helping people, entertaining them or teaching them something new that has the potential to change their life!

While all of that is tremendous, during those periods of change and reinventing yourself, the steep highs tend to make the lows look much lower. You may be able to relate this to the highs and lows in your life. One moment things are going great, you've got cash in hand and food on the table, then WHAM! something comes along to knock you to the ground again.

You know, all this up and down has taught me one thing: Losers get knocked down and stay down. Winners are winners because if they get knocked down 9 times, they get back up 10 times!

Listen, I know things may be tough right now, but you are a winner. I know you are or you wouldn't be reading this report. I congratulate you for all you are doing to get some positive forward motion going again... don't allow your fire, your passion, to go out. Remember, doing something is much better than standing still. At least when you are moving, you have positive motion and you can always course correct to keep things on track!

After years of education, having my own successful businesses, and even trying working for someone else, I finally realized something that was life changing for me. I have to follow my passion, my true calling, to be happy with myself and to feel as if I have made a difference in this world. Otherwise, what is the point to riding this big rock around in space for all these years?

HOW TO GET (AND KEEP) MORE MONEY and EDDIE POWELL'S QUANTUM LEAP BUSINESS TRAINING © 2010 Shared Resource Network, Inc., POB 65, Reynoldsburg, OH 43068-0065 USA   All World Rights Reserved. 8
Eddie@EddiePowell.com

I know you know that feeling, too. You also know that if you are not on course, not centered within your "significant space", you feel like you have fallen off a really high cliff and you are just waiting for the very big thud at the end that you know is coming.

Well, enough of that! Today is the day that I would like to share with you The 3 Secret Keys of How To Get (And Keep) More Money. These are the ones I discovered after many ups and downs, after doing some very intensive soul searching and asking God to help me turn all this financial mess around. These are the answers He gave me and now, I am sharing them with you and the world!

With your permission, let's dive right in…

The first key is to develop a healthy respect for money as a tool. It is not something to be coveted, to be jealous of someone else having more of it than you, or to seek above all else. Those are paths to strife, family problems, negative emotions that will overtake and drown you in a sea of dark confusion. You can love people, you should never love money, it is a cruel taskmaster.

A healthy respect for money includes several things. A knowing that money is nothing more than a means of barter, of exchange, to facilitate the purchase and use of goods and services by one person from another person, instead of the old methods of trading a cow for some corn meal, for instance, it is simply much easier to carry some paper and coins to the exchange location.

Money must be owned the same way that you own a hammer, a saw, a table, a chair. Money is so emotional – when you don't have it, you need it – but when you have it, it is very easy for it to have you. I maintain that your happiness and joy must come from personal choice as in choosing to be happy, not from some material thing, even money.

Since money is the welcomed means of exchange in the world, then it makes sense

Eddie@EddiePowell.com

to have some but do not let it taint your decisions, your job, your relationships, for money is fleeting. In other words, when you have money, you will have many friends (some that crawl out of the woodwork, it seems), yet when money moves on, so do your supposed friends.

You may have been raised in an environment where you were taught not to discuss money, politics, and religion. In many cases, since money was not discussed nor the means to acquire it, use it, and save it, many of us are ill equipped to handle it. So, get some books, talk with accountants, bankers, and others that are more in-tune with money, how it flows, and all that that entails.

Most importantly, start imagining yourself with money. Money for food, rent, cars, clothes, homes, and all the things that you have not allowed yourself to think about like vacations, second homes in vacation spots, trips to see relatives, businesses you would like to create and more. While some of these things are for you, remember to envision some things to help other people. These thoughts will serve to supercharge your thinking and make the money move faster on your behalf as you recognize the works you can do with money.

The second of the three keys of how to get (and keep) more money is to commit yourself to adding value to other people. This is accomplished fastest by starting a business. Simply stated, buying a product then making it available to a consumer is a great way to add value through convenience. Another way is to start with an idea or product of someone else's, add something to it, then charging more for it because it provides an even greater value to the consumer. Packaging information into bite-sized chucks that are more easily consumed by the client is another way to generate improved value and thus, command extra money.

Your own business also allows you to keep more money before taxes by allowing certain write-off's, business expenses, and tax advantages. For instance, a real estate professional from Central Ohio is required to review a property in Florida for consideration of sale or purchase for a client. The journey's expenses could possibly become a tax write-off for the real estate business (please consult a reputable tax professional for advice in such situations for your own business).

Such things as hiring your children, car expenses, a portion of your home expenses for having a home-office, uniforms, professional subscriptions, internet access, cell phones and more could become items to be considered for deductions from your own business, depending upon your business structure and operations (again, this is where a reputable tax professional plays an important role).

Remember, your business can range from a solo-entrepreneurship to multiple people working to build your business. While it will be important to consult a legal professional for advice on the business organizational choices, you may well find an option best suited to you, your business dreams and vision for the future. Having your own business is one of the better ways to get more money and keep more money. Please investigate things completely before jumping in.

The third and final key of how to get and keep more money is tithing. Tithing is a Bible-based principle that instructs the person to return 10 percent of their income to the storehouse where they are getting their faith built and spirit renewed.

While God does not need your money, He does want your commitment. He wants to see your heart and if you will follow instruction. Follow His instruction and prove that you can be trusted in little things then you will be rewarded with even greater things.

This is a testing compared to when you let your children learn to drive. First, you allowed them to drive with you in the car. They did fine and passed the testing, so you allowed them to drive down the block to the store. Slowly, you tested and allowed a little more. Eventually, your child could borrow the car and drive it across country without huge concerns on your part. God tests and proves us, too. Greater rewards are yours as you continue to be trusted.

There you have it, The 3 Secret Keys of How To Get (And Keep) More Money. I encourage you to focus and engage every step to receive more and more rewards in your life. With that said, I can also tell you that you will be challenged to stay focused. Things will crowd your schedule, emergencies will change your focus, and trials will make you wonder and doubt your choices.

Stay the course, make adjustments, but stay the course. If you are not moving and become stuck, all forward motion will be lost and any positive results will disappear. You will soon be back to counting baloney slices, eating beans and noodle dinners, and looking for options of a place to rest your head. Sure, challenges will take the shape of cars, kids, finances, and even the voices in your head that continue to tell you success is not anywhere in your future!

Focus on your ultimate objective, money for your family, your business, your home, your retirement, even money for your school, your church, or to help someone else.

While starting a new business may feel like uncharted territory, it is vital to your small business success to get some business training, move your mindset, and reshape your destiny. Your future is not locked to your past. You do not have to accept past failures as your future.

Trust me, I have been on this journey, too. I learned at a young age to turn my hobby into a financial opportunity, moving from a basement operation to traveling the United States and Canada, recording, authoring, training, and sharing my gifts of entertainment with millions throughout my career. This entertainment career opened the door into radio and eventually television as an on-air personality, producer, syndication

HOW TO GET (AND KEEP) MORE MONEY and EDDIE
POWELL'S QUANTUM LEAP BUSINESS TRAINING © 2010
Shared Resource Network, Inc., POB 65, Reynoldsburg, OH 43068-
0065 USA   All World Rights Reserved. 16
Eddie@EddiePowell.com

expert, and promoter. Marketing, copywriting, advertising and several awards later then shifted into education and training with corporate training, speaking, coaching, focused on workforce and business development program creation and operation.

Today, this has all morphed into the expert status I now enjoy, having been recognized with the U.S. Small Business Administration 2007 Journalist of the Year award, Region V; a U.S. Congressional Order of Merit; a U.S. Presidential Commission from President George W. Bush; inclusion in *Who's Who in Entertainment, Who's Who in Finance and Industry, Who's Who in America,* and *Who's Who in the World,* among others.

I have been fortunate enough to work on several highly valued projects from the U.S. Department of Labor, partner with organizations including CVS/Caremark, Ohio Department of Job & Family Services, AmVets, Allied CDL Training Systems, Robert Half International, Lee Hecht

Harrison, and Suzuki of America, along with many broadcast, print, and Internet media outlets. Walmart, Kroger, Wendy's, Arby's, Max & Erma's, Golden Corral, USPS, Dairy Queen, and many others have been Sponsor Partners in projects developed by Shared Resource Network, Inc., our not-for-profit educational arm.

Membership programs count AmVets, Volunteers of America, The Columbus Dispatch Group, PNC, Chase, Huntington, Alliance Data, The Gap Brands, National Church Residencies, Jewish Family Services, Urban League, United Way of Central Ohio, and nearly 600 other active community leadership organizations as members. I have served on Boards of Goodwill, COTA, Community Housing Network, Community Economic Development – Aberdeen, Ohio, and others, as I focus a good portion of my time and energy on giving back to produce additional positive results in the world.

Now, I am delighted to help you, personally!

I have heard from many people that as you seek to engage in applying The 3 Secret Keys of How To Get (And Keep) More Money in your life, the challenge is how to start your own business. They have not been in a position in life to study and learn the information necessary to be successful.

The U.S. Small Business Administration compiles and distributes statistics. One of those that completely devastates me is that 90 percent of all U.S. Small Businesses started this year will fail within One Year. In addition, of those remaining 90 percent of those will fail within the following Four Years!

My heart goes out to them for I know that they need proper information and encouragement. These folks were unprepared. Perhaps they had a good idea but did not understand how to market and

Eddie@EddiePowell.com

sell their products. Could be that they did not research the market well to determine the potential success of their idea. Some probably tried to apply the old adage about building a better mousetrap and they will come, only to find that stocking a store and opening the doors for business does not bring customers nor sales without focused effort!

While I may not be able to help too many of them, I can provide this valuable information and training to YOU!

Eddie Powell's Quantum Leap Business Training© will provide the foundational support you need to get started on the right foot.

> ### *Change is the constant companion of Time.*
> ### *– Eddie Powell*

What Do You See For Your Future?

It Is Time To Take Action, To Grab Your Success!

I congratulate you for making it this far...

You are evidencing the necessary desire, passion, and commitment to move forward in a big way with a business of your own...

It is your personal focus, ability to do the right thing, and willingness to work hard and smart, coupled with the right knowledge and team, that will bring you to ultimate success!

Do not end up like so many other former business owners...

After a couple of weeks, you aren't yet seeing any results. It's feeling a bit tough and quite honestly, you're getting board already. Meanwhile, you get hit up with another opportunity and this one really does seem too good to pass up. So you ignore your better judgment and take a different focus for your business, yet again.

Before too long you're actually feeling pretty overwhelmed. You've spent all this money, you aren't seeing results, and you're spending 8, 10, maybe 12 hours a day behind your counter trying to focus on your business feeling quite frustrated.

So what we end up with is a desperate situation with symptoms like these:

- Lack of focus

- Too many opportunities

- Too many conflicting choices

- Information overload

- Inefficient use of time

- Analysis paralysis

- Daydreaming

- Not setting realistic goals

- Procrastination

- Perfectionism

- Fear of failure

- Lack of self belief

- Desperation

- Impatience

- Shortcuts

- Magic bullets

and so the cycle continues...

It's like trying to ride a bike when the chain has come off...

won't get you very far!

It Is Time You Get Out Of The Rat Race,

Learn How To Get (And Keep) More Money,

And

Gain Unstoppable Momentum For

YOUR OWN BUSINESS!

IN BUSINESS FOR YOURSELF NOT BY YOURSELF

Eddie Powell's Exclusive Quantum Leap Business Training©

10 Distinct Interactive Business Modules

Each Presented With A

Hands-On Real World Approach

By

Industry Leading

Knowledge Experts

You can expect my personal involvement as we present and deliver insights and information straight from the front line of hands-on real world businesses. These are proven strategies that can leap your business ahead without having to suffer all the struggles and opportunities for failure so many other businesses encounter.

Mindsets based on experience, strategies and perspectives targeting results. Eddie Powell's Quantum Leap Business Training© will provide the tools to get your business started quickly...

Imagine a car... won't run without fuel, right? Well, we help you get the right vehicle. Then, you simply supply the fuel energy and steer in the correct direction to achieve your personal success!

Here's what you will get in this exclusive 10 Module Package:

Module One

The Foundation Of Business

Six Pillars Of Every Business

Are You Ready To Be A Business Owner?

Products and Services: Give The Market What It Wants

Delivering Exceptional Customer Satisfaction

Module Two

Marketing For Money

How Do I Meet You?

Why Should I Trust You?

WIIFM: What's In It For Me

Fickle Consumers + Global Opportunities

Module Three

Keeping It Real, Keeping It Legal

Business Structure

You Are Going To Need A Lawyer On Your Team

FAQ's

Module Four

Counting The Money

What You Need To Know To Keep Your Accountant Honest

Tax Time

Insuring Your Future

FAQ's

Module Five

Help, Help: Hiring, Getting Free Help, Selection

Building Your Empire

Strategies & Objectives

The Art Of War: You & Your Competition – Friends Or Foes?

Module Six

SWOT Analysis

Systems and Processes: Flow

Operations: Constraint Theory

A Finely Tuned Instrument Of Capitalism

Module Seven

A Little Less Talk & A Lot More Action!

Doing Business: Individual Reports From
The Field

Overcoming Fears & Claiming Results

Reaching For The Stars

Module Eight

Getting Launched: Up & Running

Media, PR, & Making Breaking News

Let No Crisis Go Unheralded

Corporate Social Responsibility (CSR)

Module Nine

Branding Brilliance

Networking Know-How

Be Unique (Like The Rest Of Us)

OUTSTANDING!

Module Ten

Embrace The Future: Change & Time

To Walk On Water – Get Out Of The Boat

Red Ocean – Blue Ocean: Re-invent + Re-Purpose

A Thinking Mind: Change & Mindset

What Business Means To You

Now is the time to put yourself in the top 2% of people by making a commitment to yourself that the responsibility for Getting and Keeping More Money is firmly on your shoulders. It is down to you and you alone. Your own business is a key and you can do it with help!

Remember, Life owes us absolutely nothing. We need to stop passing the buck and pointing the finger at other people, and just accept that it is down to each of us... alone... to try, to succeed, and to get and keep more money!

Please, let me share this with you, some people are too scared to take this step…

But, I have to tell you, having the courage to take full responsibility for yourself and your success is incredibly empowering. You no longer have to sit around hoping that the perfect simple easy system will land in your in-box or that you might win the lottery one day.

After you finish Eddie Powell's Quantum Leap Business Training© you will find yourself asking better questions and being much clearer about what it is you really want to achieve with your life.

Think about it. Each of us is given a set number of days to do what we were set upon the earth to do and to accomplish our purpose. Then, our ticket is punched and we gain a new place of residence on the other side.

<u>You can look at it this way, If the average life expectancy is:</u>

78 years for females in the United States

and

76 years for males in the United States

Translated, that means

Females have 28,470 days on average on earth

and

Males have 27,740 days on average

Assuming that the first 20 years of your life was spent learning typical operational stuff like language, math, and relationship stuff

That means that roughly 7,300 days were used up learning

and leaves only

Females 21,170 days

and

Males 20,440 days

to accomplish their Purpose in Life

Now, for **YOU** personally...

Simply subtract 20 from your current age

Then, take that number and multiply by 365 days in a year...

Got it?

Now, take that number and subtract it from

21,170 if you are Female

or

20,440 days if you are Male

What is this new number you have uncovered?

That is the approximate number of days you have left on earth, given common statistics and assuming relatively good health.

Now, obviously, no one but God knows for sure and

you could be involved in an accident or hit by lightning, for instance,

critically shortening your life span...

But, for sake of this material, I have chosen this method to illustrate a

very important point...

Every day you waste is a day off your total...

Every day you put off trying to achieve your Purpose in Life,

is another day gone, that you will never again recover, and

puts you that much further from your goal...

So, let me ask you this:

IS TODAY THE DAY YOU NEED TO START YOUR OWN BUSINESS?

IS TODAY THE DAY THAT YOU DECIDE TO START GOING FOR

YOUR GOAL AND PURPOSE?

IS TODAY THE DAY YOU STOP MAKING EXCUSES,

STOP PROCRASTINATING...

...REALLY FOCUS ON BEING ALL YOU WERE MEANT TO BE?

IF YOU SAID YES TO ANY OF THOSE QUESTIONS,

THEN

HERE IS YOUR NEXT STEP...

SIMPLY EMAIL YOUR CONTACT INFORMATION TO:

Eddie@EddiePowell.com

Enter Your Contact Information Including Valid Email You Will Gain Access To Our Information On Upcoming Trainings:

Eddie@EddiePowell.com

Eddie Powell's

Quantum Leap Business Training(c)

So You Can Understand

HOW TO GET (AND KEEP) MORE MONEY©

*All of Eddie Powell's Trainings
are offered in a variety of media formats
including:
live seminars, workshops, bootcamps,
corporate retreats, college presentations,
DVD, CD, eBooks, Online, and more for
your convenience.*

Contact: Eddie@EddiePowell.com
to arrange speaking engagements.

WE REPECT AND HONOR YOUR TIME - THANK YOU!

www.ingramcontent.com/pod-product-compliance
Lightning Source LLC
Chambersburg PA
CBHW061232180526
45170CB00003B/1268